T0123611

THE PRACTICAL STRATEGIES SERIES
IN GIFTED EDUCATION

series editors
FRANCES A. KARNES & KRISTEN R. STEPHENS

Reading for Gifted Students

Elizabeth A. Fogarty, Ph.D.

NEW YORK AND LONDON

First published 2012 by Prufrock Press Inc.

Published 2021 by Routledge
605 Third Avenue, New York, NY 10017
2 Park Square, Milton Park, Abingdon, Oxon OX14 4RN

Routledge is an imprint of the Taylor & Francis Group, an informa business

ISBN 13: 978-1-59363-892-4 (pbk)

Contents

Series Preface

The Practical Strategies Series in Gifted Education offers teachers, counselors, administrators, parents, and other interested parties up-to-date instructional techniques and information on a variety of issues pertinent to the field of gifted education. Each guide addresses a focused topic and is written by an individual with authority on the issue. Several guides have been published. Among the titles are:

- *Acceleration Strategies for Teaching Gifted Learners*
- *Curriculum Compacting: An Easy Start to Differentiating for High-Potential Students*
- *Enrichment Opportunities for Gifted Learners*
- *Independent Study for Gifted Learners*
- *Motivating Gifted Learners*
- *Questioning Strategies for Teaching the Gifted*
- *Social & Emotional Teaching Strategies*

For a current listing of available guides within the series, please visit Prufrock Press at http://www.prufrock.com.

Introduction

> I knew nothing except what I gathered from *Time* magazine and reading everything I could lay hands on at home, but as I inched sluggishly along the treadmill of the Maycomb County school system, I could not help receiving the impression that I was being cheated out of something.
>
> —Jean Louise "Scout" Finch in *To Kill a Mockingbird* (Lee, 1960)

In her 1960 novel, Harper Lee writes about Scout Finch, a precocious youth who is the prototype of a gifted reader. Having taught herself, Scout enters school able to read—much to the chagrin of her teacher, who tells Scout to stop reading at home. Unfortunately, the experiences of Scout Finch parallel those of many gifted readers who sit unchallenged in classrooms day after day.

Reading achievement continues to be the most important factor in school success for readers at all ability levels (Anderson, Hiebert, Scott, & Wilkinson, 1985; Daneman, 1996; National Reading Panel, 2000). Without a strong reading foundation, students often cannot comprehend content-specific texts and therefore experience difficulty even in areas of strength, such as science and math. Any definition of reading must include not only decoding, but comprehension as well. Therefore, reading can be defined as an active process in which an existing schema is used to facilitate comprehension through the decoding of text in order to create meaning. Preoccupation with making sure that students are mastering basic reading skills to the detriment of teaching higher level thinking and problem solving, however, can detract from the ability of gifted readers to make continuous progress. Thus, many gifted readers who enter first grade reading on a fifth-grade level may leave fifth grade having made little growth. Gifted readers, like other gifted students, need challenging opportunities that enable them to learn something new each day.

Gifted Readers: A Definition

Typically, gifted readers are those who read at least 2 years ahead of their chronological grade placement (Catron & Wingenbach, 1986; Dole & Adams, 1983; Tomlinson, 1999). These students vary in their learning styles and preferences but have instructional needs that differ from their nongifted peers (Catron & Wingenbach, 1986). There are several characteristics that set gifted readers apart. First, these students are likely to have extensive vocabularies and advanced language skills (Clark, 1979; Greenlaw & McIntosh, 1986; Reis et al., 2003; Reis et al., 2004). Gifted readers are more likely to use a variety of strategies to comprehend text when they read than their nongifted peers who tend to have few strategies at their disposal (Wingenbach, 1983). Fluency is another hallmark of gifted readers, as they have been known to devour books.

Additionally, gifted readers view reading differently than their peers. Reis et al. (2004) found that most gifted readers enjoyed the process of reading, perhaps because they are able to read easily and with automaticity. Gifted readers tend to be avid readers and often prefer nonfiction, how-to books, biographies, and other genres that satisfy their curiosity about the world (Richards, 2008). Nongifted readers, on the other hand, cited reading as a way to get information, rather than a pleasurable activity (Bartelo & Cornette, 1982).

Precocious Reading

Precocious readers are those children who read ahead of the predicted developmental timeline. Typically, children begin to decipher the patterns of letters that form words around the middle of kindergarten, and although the timeline varies slightly by individual, most youngsters are on their way to reading short words sometime in first grade. Precocious readers, on the other hand, crack the code early. Sometimes self-taught, these young readers seem to recognize letter patterns earlier than their chronological peers. Precocious readers typically also have advanced verbal and reasoning ability.

Although scores vary, the average IQ for a precocious reader is 130 (Jackson, 1992). Jackson (1992) further noted that this puts about half of early readers above the typical IQ cut score for gifted identification and about half below. Therefore, some precocious readers may be considered gifted in a general domain, while others might be found to have more specific reading gifts.

Although some gifted readers are considered precocious and are fully able to read at the onset of kindergarten, other gifted readers may display precocity, but do not always read earlier than classmates (Burns, Roe, & Ross, 1984; Reis et al., 2004; Terman,

1925). This suggests that even students who have not had a rich early home literacy experience can demonstrate giftedness in reading. Therefore, whereas nurturing reading development in rich literary environments may account for the early reading of some children, it does not fully account for the early development of some students in which the achievement gap between chronological age peers continues.

Teachers may need to employ creative assessment opportunities for young gifted readers because regular paper-and-pencil tests may be too sophisticated and fail to yield valid results. One teacher learned this during a conversation at her fall parent/teacher conference. When Joey's parents came to the conference, they inquired about how their son had been doing in kindergarten. The teacher indicated that he was doing fine—he was a pleasant young man, a good listener, and a joy to have in class. The teacher went on to explain that the class had been learning the letter of the week and had already worked on recognizing five letters. The teacher indicated that Joey was a good participant in the lessons. At this point in the conference, the parents exchanged glances. His father asked the teacher whether she had heard Joey read. The teacher indicated that she had never heard him read, and the parents went on to disclose that he had been reading since he was 3 years old and could read picture books as well as beginning chapter books.

As it turns out, Joey was afraid to tell his teacher he could read for fear of hurting her feelings. Instead, he opted to blend in with the other learners, sacrificing challenge in order to fit in. After their conference, Joey's teacher moved him to a first-grade reading class where he was able to get the challenge that he needed.

Early grades teachers should utilize information provided by parents as much as possible when getting to know students. Sending home surveys where parents can indicate their child's abilities is a great way to learn more about young students. Kindergarten teachers especially have an opportunity to gather this information when children and their parents visit the school for the prekindergarten screening. While teachers are administering performance indicators such as reading readiness assessments to children, parents can be providing information about their child's strengths and talents. Knowing that students can read at the onset of kindergarten can help teachers make grouping decisions, such as placing all readers into one kindergarten classroom where the teacher can provide additional challenge (see Grouping, pp. 19–22, for more information).

Identifying Gifted Readers

In addition to the conditions previously mentioned about precocious readers, gifted readers often go unrecognized in regular classrooms due to testing limitations that make it difficult for these students to be acknowledged. Testing limitations can exist in all types of tests, including those that are teacher-created, from the basal reading series, or are statewide criterion-referenced and national standardized reading tests. The limited scope of a teacher-created test, for example, may make it difficult for teachers to see the breadth and depth of students' knowledge. One benefit of teacher-created tests, however, is that they can be used frequently to gauge students' knowledge and provide justification for compacting the curriculum (see Differentiating for Gifted Readers, pp. 16–29, for more information). Like a teacher-created test, a test from the basal series will be limited to grade-level content and will not allow for the demonstration of mastery beyond the scope of the basal series curriculum. Criterion-referenced statewide tests are similarly limited in that grade-level curriculum is tested; however, these tests do have a greater range of tested content. Even national standardized tests can be problematic in that ceiling effects can limit the amount of usable information that can be gained. Off-level testing, such as having a second-grade student take the third-grade test, can provide more information about student weaknesses and areas where further instruction is needed. These tests can also demonstrate how well students would be able to fare on advanced curricula, thus providing a justification for the use of curriculum compacting. Finally, national standardized tests also provide for comparison among students across grade levels through the use of scaled scores.

Additional assessment types can also be used to assist teachers in making decisions about students who may benefit from differentiated services. These can be less formal than the tests mentioned previously and can include skills checklists, observations, interviews, running records, or interest inventories (more information on alternate assessments can be found in VanTassel-Baska, 2008).

Lack of Challenge

Talented students often do not receive challenging instruction and instead are asked to complete work that is too simple and redundant for them (Archambault et al., 1993; Reis et al., 2004; Reis, Westberg, Kulikowich, & Purcell, 1998; Westberg, Archambault, Dobyns, & Salvin, 1993). In a 1993 study by Westberg and colleagues, no differentiation was provided to gifted and talented students during 84% of the instructional time observed. Results from a more recent study have suggested that although differentiation has become a favorite topic of professional development discussions, few teachers are making such practices regular and substantive for gifted learners (Fogarty, 2011). It is important, however, for gifted learners to encounter challenging experiences so they may grow.

Gifted readers may be the most underchallenged students in the regular classroom. Observational studies have shown that teachers of reading rarely vary their instruction to include more challenging content or materials (Reis et al., 2003; Richards, 2003). Although teachers may use forms of grouping in reading classrooms, such as guided reading groups or ability groups, the instruction in these groups is often not a great deal different from

Table 1
Frequently Used Reading Classroom Practices

	Average Readers	Talented Readers
Reading nonfiction books	x	x
Choosing interest-based books	x	x
Connecting to prior knowledge	x	x
Finding deeper meaning in their reading	x	x
Demonstrating comprehension in assessment and class work	x	x
Reading above-grade-level books		x
Using reading lists from higher grade levels		x
Reflecting on their reading		x
Developing and applying new ideas		x

Note. These categories represent practices that teachers self-reported using (4) *usually* and (5) *consistently* in their classrooms on the Current Classroom Practices for Reading scale (Richards, 2003).

that used with the rest of the class, thus providing no real differentiation. Recent classroom observations have indicated that the basal reading textbook continues to be the dominant mode of instruction for reading in the elementary grade classroom (Fogarty, 2006). In middle-grades classrooms, reading textbooks are often used alongside class novel sets. However, the use of a single text for all students in the class is problematic in that no one text can adequately challenge all learners at one grade level.

Richards's (2003) survey further illustrated the fact that gifted readers typically receive the same instruction provided to all learners. Teachers were asked to respond to 30 survey items indicating the degree to which certain instructional practices were used with average and talented readers (see Table 1). Aside from four strategies that were used more often with talented readers, most of the instructional practices were found to be used equally often with average and talented readers.

In a similar study conducted in the same year (Reis et al., 2003), observational data from 12 third- and seventh-grade classrooms paint a similarly bleak picture about the lack of differentiation for gifted readers in regular classrooms.

Although the data in Tables 1 and 2 do not examine the practices of teachers of the gifted, it is important to understand that the gifted readers involved in these studies spent most or all of their instructional day in the regular classroom setting. Unfortunately, the findings of the researchers cited in Tables 1 and 2 mirror findings from a study conducted 10 years earlier by Westberg and colleagues (1993), which revealed that little differentiation was provided to gifted students. In a follow-up study, this author sought to determine whether the interest in differentiation in the mid-2000s would affect classroom practice. Findings revealed little evidence, however, that there is any more differentiation going on today than when the original study was conducted nearly 20 years ago (Fogarty, 2011).

Table 2
Reading Instruction for Talented Readers

	Teachers Using the Strategy	
Methods of Instructional Differentiation	*n*	% of sample
Curriculum compacting to eliminate work that students had already mastered and replace with challenging options	3	25
Within-class grouping for interest or for more challenging activities	3	25
Use of more advanced instruction for groups and individual students	3	25
Use of higher level questioning skills	3	25
Availability of advanced materials	3	25
Gifted pull-out program opportunities during reading or language arts	3	25
Use of classroom libraries with advanced, challenging books	3	25
Integrated enrichment opportunities	3	25
Use of talented readers as role models or group discussion leaders	2	17
Use of technology during reading class	1	8
Replacement of Success for All/direct instruction with standard literature program	2	17

Note. The table above gives data from a study involving observations in the classrooms of 12 teachers of grades 3 and 7. Adapted from "Reading Instruction for Talented Readers: Case Studies Documenting Few Opportunities for Continuous Progress" (RM 03184), by S. M. Reis et al., 2003, Storrs: University of Connecticut, The National Research Center on the Gifted and Talented. Copyright 2003 by The National Research Center on the Gifted and Talented.

Differentiating for Gifted Readers

Effective differentiated instruction for gifted readers may involve modifications to the curriculum, varied grouping arrangements, and alternative activities, but teachers should facilitate differentiation options, rather than provide only independent work for gifted readers. Differentiation for the gifted reader can occur when the content, process, product, or environment is varied. A list of recommended practices for use with gifted readers is shown in Table 3. Teachers can also take into consideration Kingore's "The Gifted Reader's Bill of Rights" when designing learning opportunities for gifted children (see Appendix A).

Materials can enhance or inhibit teachers' ability to differentiate. Basal reading textbooks, although often used in reading classrooms, may make it difficult for teachers to provide substantive differentiation. In a typical fifth-grade classroom, for instance, a teacher may have some students reading at the second-grade level while gifted readers in the same classroom may be reading at a post-high-school level. In a classroom where the reading levels of the students span 10 grade levels, a single textbook is not likely to provide reading passages and activities

Table 3
Suggested Practices for Use With Gifted Readers

Recommended Strategy	Author(s)
Encouraged to read books on a wide variety of topics	Clark, 2002; Richards, 2003
Encouraged to read books in areas of their interest	Dole & Adams, 1983; Richards, 2003
Exposure to advanced vocabulary	Howell, 1985; Richards, 2003
Elimination of previously mastered curriculum; use of advanced-level work	Reis, Burns, & Renzulli, 1992; Renzulli, 1977; Renzulli & Reis, 1985, 1997
Exposure to higher level thinking skills	Dole & Adams, 1983; Kaplan, 2001; Parker, 1998; VanTassel-Baska & Brown, 2001
Grouped with like-ability peers	Dole & Adams, 1983; Gentry, 1999; Kulik & Kulik, 1991; Levande, 1999; Rogers, 1991
Subject acceleration	Colangelo, Assouline, & Gross, 2004

appropriate for everyone; some will struggle to understand the text and others will be left unchallenged. In a survey of average and gifted fifth- and sixth-grade readers, teachers used basal readers 100% of the time with average readers and 99% of the time with gifted readers (Marion, 1982). These data are 30 years old; however, recent research suggests that although textbooks are not as popular as they once were, they are still used frequently in reading instruction (Fogarty, 2006).

Another commonly occurring practice in the elementary reading classroom is the use of guided reading. A form of differentiated instruction, guided reading allows teachers to meet with small groups of children whose reading levels are similar in order to provide instruction on specific skills and strategies. During a guided reading lesson, the teacher typically begins by introducing a group of about six students to a text at their instructional reading level (material that can be read with assistance) and previewing the text with them. Once the students and the teacher have previewed the text, specific skills may be taught that students will utilize while reading. As students commence reading, the teacher listens to each read quietly and may ask comprehension questions or offer strategy suggestions to students.

Guided reading is widely regarded by reading experts to be an effective way to provide instruction to elementary reading students. Although it is an effective and scientifically based practice, it may not fully meet the needs of gifted readers. One challenge with this method is that it is based on providing the same instruction to a small group of students. Even when narrowed from an entire class to about six students, the needs of the students in the group are still likely to differ from the needs of a truly *gifted* reader. This may be particularly true in that the guided reading level of the group may differ from the one or two gifted readers present in the group. Alternately, the gifted reader may be able to effectively use a greater number of reading strategies when encountering text than a nongifted peer. Therefore, even in a differentiated group, the gifted reader may require sufficiently different instruction. Teachers are cautioned to utilize guided reading groups with gifted readers on an as-needed basis, occurring more often in the primary grades than the intermediate grades and decreasing in frequency as demonstrable differences between gifted readers and their peers appear.

One alternative to using guided reading is to convene gifted readers to read and discuss texts from the Junior Great Books series. This series provides quality literature as well as open-ended discussion questions to encourage rich conversations and higher order thinking.

One way that teachers can increase the relevance and rigor in classrooms is to base curriculum on big ideas—curricular themes that can be universally applied to many content areas. Common examples of big ideas include change, conflict, exploration, force or influence, identity, order versus chaos, patterns, power, structure, systems, and relationships. When conducting a novel study, for instance, reading teachers can look for how *power* or *relationships* are related to the motivations of the characters or the plot sequence. There are several William and Mary Literature Units available from the Center for Gifted Education at The College of William and Mary that allow teachers to do just that. In the *Journeys and Destinations* unit, for example, students study both change and relationships to understand the place of humans in the world.

Looking at curriculum from a wide lens, as with these big ideas, allows teachers to incorporate more abstract ideas, such as comparing the relationships among characters in a novel. Alternately, teachers can integrate complexity during a study of several texts as students examine how the balance of power between men and women has changed over time as evidenced in fiction writing. Integrating several themes throughout the school year and across several content areas can allow teachers to demonstrate interrelatedness throughout the curriculum (Erickson, 2007).

Grouping

Flexible grouping is an important component of an appropriately differentiated program for gifted learners. Negative stigmas associated with ability grouping have caused some teachers to shy away from grouping practices and can create a roadblock for effective differentiation (Cohen, 1997). In fact, Richards' (2003) work has shown that 70% of teachers in grades 3–7 do not use any form of grouping in their reading and language arts instruction.

Several researchers have noted that the use of flexible grouping arrangements, along with appropriately differentiated instruction, have been shown to be effective for students of all ability levels (Renzulli, 1994; Tomlinson, 1999). Varying the environment under which students receive their instruction is one way to differentiate.

There are several forms of grouping that are appropriate for use with gifted readers. The first, which is also the most extreme, is acceleration. This can be considered a form of grouping in that students are grouped with their intellectual or like-ability peers, rather than their age peers. Grade-level acceleration involves moving a student to the next grade level for more advanced instruction and benefits students with multiple strength areas (Colangelo et al., 2004). The Iowa Acceleration Scale is commercially available and can be used to determine whether grade-level acceleration is appropriate (Assouline, Colangelo, Lupkowski-Shoplik, Forstadt, & Lipscomb, 2003).

Subject acceleration, on the other hand, can be used when students display advanced skills in a specific area. For instance, a student who displays advanced reading ability in the third grade could be subject accelerated in order to attend a fourth-grade reading class. When implementing subject acceleration, it is important that schools make a long-term plan for how a student will be served across a number of years. Thus, there should be a viable option for the fifth grader who has been subject accelerated in a K–5 school. Allowing a student to attend a local middle school part time is one way that schools have addressed this challenge.

Across-grade grouping is another way that gifted readers can be grouped to provide differentiated services. One form of across-grade grouping is cluster grouping in which several gifted students are clustered into one classroom with a specially trained teacher. When clustered together, it has been found that gifted students make more growth than their nongifted peers taught outside of clustered classrooms (Gentry, 1999). Unlike a self-contained gifted classroom, students of average and below-average ability are also assigned to the classroom, but low students are excluded.

Assembling a group of gifted students helps to ensure that the teacher will serve them—it is more difficult to ignore a group of students than a single gifted student in the classroom. With only a few gifted students in their classroom, teachers may not have the time to appropriately serve these students. Rather than trying to meet a wide variety of student needs, a teacher in a cluster-grouped class is working to meet the needs of students in three primary groupings: high achieving (gifted), average, and below average. In another classroom, then, a teacher may have a group of above-average students, average students, and below-average students. Although the range of abilities may shift, cluster grouping shrinks the range of abilities present in each classroom, making it more possible for teachers to meet the needs of all learners present.

Research on cluster grouping has shown that positive results have been found not only for gifted students, but for students at other ability levels as well. For instance, Gentry (1999) found that teachers identified more high achievers (gifted students) for the cluster group each year the model was used. Above-average learners began to perform better when gifted students were no longer present in their classrooms. The same held true for learners at other levels: More average students were designated as above average and more below-average students were designated as average, and it began to appear that everyone in the school was getting smarter.

Cluster grouping can be especially effective for gifted readers when the grouping assignments are based on reading ability or achievement. Schools may use students' standardized ability or achievement test scores when assigning students to clusters, but some type of measure other than grades is recommended in order to identify students with potential whose grades may be poor due to underachievement. Teacher recommendations can also be used, but administrators are advised to provide training prior to a recommendation period so that teachers can begin to recognize the differences between bright students and those who may be gifted.

A less formal method of providing across-grade grouping arrangements is to convene groups based on like ability determined by content area or subject matter. This method is particularly helpful when cluster grouping is not being used or when cluster grouping is being used but students proficient in reading are spread across several classrooms. For example, if students have been preassessed for the upcoming unit and several have shown mastery of the reading concepts, one teacher in a grade level may elect to work with a group of gifted readers from across several classrooms (see Curriculum Compacting section on the following page for more information). The teacher may provide a discussion group on a more advanced novel, advanced vocabulary study, or other type of differentiated option for the group.

Within-class flexible grouping can also be used to provide differentiated experiences for gifted readers. In this grouping format, teachers create groups from within their classrooms typically based on readiness, but groups can also be formed based on learning styles or interest. To avoid the "blue jays and buzzards" mentality that often results in inflexible reading groups, teachers are encouraged to frequently reassign membership so that children are able to move among groups as their instructional needs change. When membership becomes stagnant, or when students are relegated to a certain type of group (often the low-ability group) for long periods, they may begin to perceive that they are less able to achieve than their peers. Flexible groups can be formed based on the results of a unit-based preassessment, thus allowing students to rotate in and out of a group each time a new unit is started.

Flexible grouping arrangements enable teachers to use tiered assignments to meet the varying needs of students in a mixed-ability classroom. Tiered assignments allow teachers to teach the same concept or skill to students of varying ability levels by creating several activity tiers. Teachers can increase the abstraction, complexity, or sophistication of learning activities for students with greater readiness and can decrease the same factors for students with less readiness, all while teaching the same concept or skill. In the reading classroom, this might involve texts of differing levels or assignments that are more open-ended for one group than another.

Curriculum Compacting

Because gifted readers often enter a grade level able to read materials several years ahead of their chronological grade placement, teachers can use curriculum compacting to demonstrate what these students already know. Curriculum compacting is the process of using preassessment to determine students' prior knowledge, documenting that knowledge, and replacing the previously mastered curriculum with alternate content and activities. Studies show that even after replacing nearly 50% of the planned instruction from a unit of study with enrichment learning opportunities, gifted students will perform as well or better than their nongifted counterparts on unit postassessments (Reis et al., 1993).

Figure 1 shows an example of a completed compacting form for Kelly, a fifth-grade student, whose teacher used preassessments to determine her understanding of reading and math concepts prior to the start of each unit. The Compactor (Reis et al., 1992) documents a student's areas of strength in the first column. Therefore, if a teacher administers a preassessment and finds a student with a great deal of proficiency in reading, the teacher would go on to record how that proficiency was determined. For instance, if a student makes a particularly high score on a preassessment, the teacher might document the percentage of answers correct on the form, as in Figure 1. If a student had demonstrated proficiency through a product, on the other hand, the teacher would note the high standards that were exemplified. Finally, the far right column is for listing the alternate activities that the student will complete in lieu of the regular classroom work.

Figure 1 shows that Kelly scored a 92% and 98% on the preassessments listed. In this case, the preassessments covered both reading and language arts skills. Once Kelly's teacher documented her proficiency with the curriculum, she met with Kelly to discuss what she wanted to work on when everyone else in the class was working on the skills she had already mastered. Kelly shared with her teacher that she had been writing a novel

The Compactor

Student's Name: Kelly

Areas of Strength	Documenting Mastery	Alternate Activities
Reading/LA	91% on Theme 1 Pretest	• Attend group mini-lesson on only those activities she did not master • Spend her time finishing her novel
Math Addition/ Subtraction	91% on Chapter 2 Pretest	• Work on addend/inverse sentences with class • Did all extra activities with the class, including her project
Reading/LA	98% on Theme 2 Pretest	• Be involved in the book group on *The Birchbark House*, continue working on her novel, and attend mini-lessons on skills she has not yet mastered

Figure 1. The Compactor is the form used to document what a gifted student's areas of strength might be and how that was assessed. This Compactor was adapted from the original form (Reis et al., 1992).

and asked if she could finish her novel during class. Together Kelly and her teacher created a contract that listed Kelly's work responsibilities while she was compacted (see Figure 2) and listed the dates that she would meet with the teacher to discuss her independent work. Kelly's contract was then sent home for her parents to review.

Teachers can work with students to develop ideas for independent studies and are encouraged to do so in order to ensure that students' interests drive the projects. At times, however, gifted students may be reluctant to put forth their own ideas or may be unaware of their options when developing an independent project. In these cases, it is usually best to have a list of possibilities for replacement activities. Here are some possible alternative activities for compacted students:

Independent Work Contract

Student's Name: Kelly

Guidelines for Independent Work

Student should:

- Have all materials ready
- Have his/her work schedule
- Be on task
- Avoid directing attention to himself/herself

Description of Replacement Activity(s):

I will be working on finishing up my novel, Sassy and Jen. This novel is about a girl who has trouble making friends, but gets along well with her horse. I'm still planning out how it will end. My ultimate goal is to get the book published. I will be submitting my completed manuscript to Mrs. Holden for this independent study.

Due Date: September 28

Teacher/Student Conference Dates:

9/7 9/9 9/12 9/14 9/19 9/20 9/22 9/26

Student's Signature: Kelly Carter

Teacher's Signature: Mrs. Holden

Figure 2. Independent work contract example. This contract is for a student who has been compacted out of much of the reading and language arts work for the current unit. This form can be found in Appendix B.

- *Author study*—Individually or with others, the student can read one or more novels by a favorite author and culminate the study by writing a letter to the author.
- *Script writing*—Students can turn a section of a novel into a script for a movie or play. Students might choose to read a nonfiction book on theater arts to learn more about stage directions, blocking, and the like.
- *Novel study*—Students could use materials from the Navigators series developed by the Center for Gifted Education at The College of William and Mary. Each guide was developed to be used with a familiar children's book and more than 50 resources are available for students in grades 1–12.
- *Nonfiction study*—Students can elect to study a real-world problem of interest through reading nonfiction materials such as articles, books, and Internet resources in order to gain insight into the problem. Possible products might include a newspaper editorial, a research paper, or a proposal for action steps toward solution of a problem.

Of course, these are just a few options for developing independent studies. Teachers and their students are likely to have many more creative ideas.

It can feel like a paperwork nightmare when first learning to use curriculum compacting, but some teachers have developed some relatively easy strategies for managing everything. After administering the unit preassessment, one teacher recorded directly into her plan book which skills the students had already mastered. Figure 3, for example, shows the reading and language arts skills that Mrs. Holden expected to teach over the course of one week as listed in her planner. Next to each of the skills, she made a note of which students had been compacted and would not need to attend the lesson. In this case, only two students had been compacted out of any of the content. None of the students showed mastery of subjects and predicates, a grammar topic that had not previously been introduced to the students. Each day

Week of September 10–14				
Monday	**Tuesday**	**Wednesday**	**Thursday**	**Friday**
Sequence of Events *Kelly, Jose	Sequence of Events *Kelly, Jose	Text Organization *Kelly	Categorize and Classify *Kelly, Jose	Categorize and Classify *Kelly, Jose
Subjects and Predicates	Subjects and Predicates	Subjects and Predicates		

Figure 3. Reading and language arts skills for the week. The example shows one way that a teacher can document which students have been compacted out of lessons.

prior to the start of the lesson, Mrs. Holden simply notified any students who were compacted out that they should work on their independent work contract.

Another teacher used a similar system to document the lessons that students had been compacted out of. As a reminder to the students, the teacher indicated the lessons they were and were not attending on Post-it® Notes that students affixed to their desks (see Figure 4). In this particular case, however, the teacher developed a set of alternate activities that students in the "Compact" group completed in lieu of the on-level lesson. Creating the alternate activities effectively created a tiered lesson situation in which there was always a more advanced and complex option for students who had been compacted out of the regular curriculum. This particular teacher opted for this situation rather than creating independent work contracts because he had a classroom where nearly all of the students regularly compacted out of several skills. He determined that creating tiered lessons would enable him to better meet the needs of his students than trying to manage nearly 20 independent contracts.

My Theme Four Skills

	Compact	On-level
Inferences		x
Compare/Contrast	x	
Past tense	x	
Suffixes		X
Prefixes	x	
Plurals	x	

Figure 4. Post-it® Note showing a student which lessons she had been compacted out of and which she was scheduled to attend as whole-class lessons. From *Differentiating Within a Gifted Classroom*, by I. Byrd, 2011. Retrieved from http://www.byrdseed.com/differentiating-within-a-gifted-classroom. Copyright 2011 Byrdseed. Reprinted with permission.

Reader's Workshop

Although there are many ways to serve gifted readers, one particularly effective way is by integrating reader's workshop into a differentiated reading classroom. Reader's workshop can be effective with nearly any grade level when modified, but seems to work best with students who are independent readers (which usually occurs around second grade).

In reader's workshop, students receive a brief mini-lesson at the start of the period, and then move into a period of independent reading on self-selected material. During the independent reading time, teachers conduct conferences with individual students on their reading selections. This one-on-one conference time provides students with differentiated instructional experiences; conferences vary in that no two conferences are alike.

Teachers have also been found to offer different types of strategies and questions depending on whether they are working with low, average, or talented readers. Teachers tend to offer more strategies to low-ability readers, but do offer some strategy instruction to all readers (Fogarty, 2006).

Few research studies have attempted to study the effectiveness of the reader's workshop model because so many variables exist, making it difficult to create an experimental study. In the field of gifted education, one large-scale study has been conducted over several years on the effectiveness of this type of reading instruction in meeting the needs of gifted readers. Research on the Schoolwide Enrichment Model–Reading (SEM-R) framework has demonstrated the model to be an effective means of challenging readers of all ability levels, not just gifted readers (Reis et al., 2005; Reis et al., 2010). It is particularly interesting to note that in this study readers had very little whole-group instruction; most of the students' instruction occurred during the individualized differentiated conferences. At the beginning of each lesson, teachers delivered a Book Hook that was designed to stimulate student interest in the book being shared and to exemplify the use of a skill or strategy through the sharing of an excerpt of the text. Teachers carried the skill or strategy into their conferences differentiating as needed based on student strengths, prior knowledge, and book choice. Despite the fact that teachers often met with students only once or twice a week, often for a total of only about 5–10 minutes of instruction, students in the SEM-R treatment consistently outperformed their peers in the non-SEM-R condition (Reis et al., 2005; Reis et al., 2010). This finding is significant and suggests that targeted differentiated instruction can provide more growth than periods of nondifferentiated whole-group instruction.

Bookmatch: Finding Adequately Challenging Books

Matching gifted readers to books can be a challenging process. They may only want to read science fiction or poetry or biographies on Jimmy Carter. In these cases, it may be difficult to find a great deal of books specific enough to the reading preferences of students. To identify students' interests, it is recommended that teachers always administer a reading preferences survey at the beginning of each school year to see what kinds of books students like. A recommended survey is the Reading Interest-A-Lyzer, which can be found in Appendix C (Reis, 2009).

Educators may worry about finding books that will sufficiently challenge talented readers. It is important to remember that challenge in reading is twofold: It comes from the complexity of the language and grammatical structure, but it also comes from the complexity and richness of the ideas. Therefore, it is possible to have a book with a fairly easy readability level and a complex theme (such as *The Giver* or *The Green Book*). Likewise, there are books with difficult grammatical structures and advanced vocabulary with simplistic themes. Often the subject matter can be too mature for students even though they are able to read the words. This is the inherent difficulty in finding "challenging" books. Which type of challenge do talented readers need? Actually, they need both. What is most important, however, is that when students are reading books that are thematically complex, they should have instruction that provides complex questioning, and they should be able to discuss the material with an adult. Conferences and guided discussion groups provide the opportunity for students and teachers to discuss books.

Appendix D contains a list of some of the best children's books published that might be of interest to gifted readers. It is difficult to compose one comprehensive list that can meet the needs of all gifted readers because their interests are often specific and diverse. The grade-level recommendations are based on what would be appropriate reading material for gifted readers in that grade. There are several caveats, however, in relation to this list.

The books selected for the list in Appendix D were selected to meet the readers on that grade level through a balance of the following blend:

- readability,
- complexity of ideas, and
- appropriate content.

Sometimes a book was placed at the 6–8 grade level because the content would be too mature for the 4–5 grade group, even if the students would be able to read the words. Therefore, the interplay of those three qualities was taken into consideration when choosing and leveling the books for this list.

The final challenge in creating a list like this is that talented readers differ. What might be challenging for one student is not challenging for another. What might interest one student will not interest another. This list is meant to be a starting place for teachers when looking for books for talented readers. Some books on this list are classics; others are just good books on topics that gifted kids typically enjoy, including justice, morality, discrimination, and independence. Websites that encompass additional book lists are also included for those in search of additional options.

Summary

Meeting the needs of gifted readers requires teachers to examine their instruction with a new lens. What modifications can be made to bring challenge to the gifted reader? Perhaps content can be compacted to make room for in-depth learning opportunities. Flexible groupings can be used to give gifted readers a time to work with other gifted readers each day. Or, alternate materials, such as William and Mary Literature Units, or models, such as reader's workshop, can be used to stimulate higher level thinking and ward off boredom. Teachers should understand that many options exist; those listed in this volume are just the beginning.

Without teachers who can recognize their strengths and make educational accommodations, students may languish on the treadmill of traditional one-size-fits-all instruction described by Scout Finch in *To Kill a Mockingbird.* Such instruction is unlikely to produce gifted readers who can read critically, analyze text, and synthesize information in new and creative ways.

Until I feared I would lose it, I never loved to read. One does not love breathing.

—Scout Finch, gifted reader

Resources

Byrd, I. (2011). *Differentiating within a gifted classroom.* Retrieved from http://www.byrdseed.com/differentiating-within-a-gifted-classroom
Ian Byrd's website is a handy gem. It provides teachers with a front-row perspective of a differentiated classroom. Just a little dose of theory supports each teacher-tested strategy imparted here and provides a healthy balance of the what to do with the why to do it.

Great Books Series (Available from http://www.greatbooks.org)
The Great Books Foundation provides reading and discussion guides for kindergarten through college-aged students. Teachers receive training in Socratic questioning and Shared Inquiry methods in order to facilitate high-level thinking.

Halsted, J. W. (2009). *Some of my best friends are books: Guiding gifted readers* (3rd ed.). Scottsdale, AZ: Great Potential Press.
Reading lists for students from preschool to college honor the uniqueness of gifted readers. With lists on topics like creativity,

aloneness, and intensity, teachers of gifted readers are sure to find something for every reader.

Keene, E. O., & Zimmerman, S. (2007). *Mosaic of thought: The power of comprehension strategy instruction* (3rd ed.). Portsmouth, NH: Heinemann.

Mosaic of Thought is a must-have resource for any teacher looking to create a reflective reading experience for his or her students. Examples from conversations from a reader's workshop are interspersed throughout the text to show how conferences can create differentiated learning experiences to challenge and extend the strategy and skill use of readers.

Kingore, B. (2004). *Differentiation: Simplified, realistic, and effective: How to challenge advanced potentials in mixed-ability classrooms.* Austin, TX: Professional Associates.

This resource provides simple straightforward strategies for differentiating. The helpful forms and ready-to-use materials make this a teacher favorite.

Lesesne, T. (2003). *Making the match: The right book for the right reader at the right time.* Portland, ME: Stenhouse.

One of the most difficult things about teaching gifted readers is finding books that challenge and engage them. With multiple book lists and many strategies for choosing the right book for each reader, teachers will spend less time looking for books and more time conferencing with readers.

Masiello, T. S. (2005). *Literature links: Activities for gifted readers.* Scottsdale, AZ: Great Potential Press.

This rich resource provides teachers of the gifted with several ready-to-use novel study mini-units for gifted readers in grades 2–6. Additional activities and resources include ready-made tools for challenging gifted readers to think creatively and critically about texts.

Opitz, M. F., & Rasinski, T. V. (2008). *Goodbye round robin: 25 effective oral reading strategies*. Portsmouth, NH: Heinemann.
Classroom teachers need multiple tools at their disposal when teaching a room full of children with varying reading needs. Reading experts Opitz and Rasinski share tips for retooling the lower elementary grades classroom to include strategies other than round robin reading.

Reis, S. M. (2009). *Joyful reading: Differentiation and enrichment for successful literacy learning*. San Francisco, CA: Jossey-Bass.
Joyful Reading is a how-to-guide for using the Schoolwide Enrichment Model–Reading (SEM-R) to challenge and motivate not only gifted readers, but all readers. Similar to a reader's workshop model, the SEM-R utilizes one-on-one conferencing and open-ended reading activities as teachers help students develop their use of reading strategies in texts of their choosing.

Reis, S. M. (2009). *The joyful reading resource kit: Teaching tools, hands-on activities, and enrichment resources*. San Francisco, CA: Jossey-Bass.
The Joyful Reading Resource Kit provides resources for the reader's workshop classroom. The resource includes open-ended reading activities and topic explorations, as well as reproducibles including student reading logs, teacher planning logs, and higher order thinking bookmark questions.

Tomlinson, C. A. (2004). *How to differentiate instruction in mixed-ability classrooms* (2nd ed.). Alexandria, VA: Association for Supervision and Curriculum Development.
Tomlinson's guide is a must-have text for any classroom teacher working with learners of varying needs in the same classroom. This text offers helpful suggestions for differentiating content, process, and product, which can be extrapolated to reading content.

VanTassel-Baska, J. (Ed.). (2008). *Alternative assessments with gifted and talented students.* Waco, TX: Prufrock Press.
This valuable guide can assist teachers in understanding the value of using authentic assessments for both formative and summative assessments with gifted students. Teachers will find valuable examples after which to pattern their own assessments.

William and Mary Literature Units
(Available from http://www.kendallhunt.com)
The award-winning William and Mary Literature curriculum units provide high-quality differentiated learning opportunities for gifted students. Each unit includes a curriculum guide with background information for teachers as well as differentiation tips to provide further challenge for gifted learners.

William and Mary Navigators
(Available from http://education.wm.edu/centers/cfge)
The Navigators series is a collection of questions and activities aligned to novels that can be used with groups of students or with individuals. The series includes more than 50 guides for grades 1–12.

References

Anderson, R., Hiebert, E. H., Scott, J., & Wilkinson, I. (Eds.). (1985). *Becoming a nation of readers* (Contract No. 400-83-0057). Washington, DC: National Institute of Education.

Archambault, F. A., Westberg, K. L., Brown, S. W., Hallmark, B. W., Emmons, E. L., & Zhang, W. (1993). *Regular classroom practices with gifted students: Results of a national survey of classroom teachers* (RM 93102). Storrs: University of Connecticut, The National Research Center on the Gifted and Talented.

Assouline, S., Colangelo, N., Lupkowski-Shoplik, A., Forstadt, L., & Lipscomb, J. (2003). *Iowa acceleration scale: A guide for whole-grade acceleration K–8* (3rd ed.). Scottsdale, AZ: Great Potential Press.

Bartelo, D. M., & Cornette, J. H. (1982, July). *A literature program for the gifted: Gifted writers + gifted readers = positive reading attitudes.* Paper presented at the International Reading Association World Congress on Reading, Dublin, Ireland.

Burns, P., Roe, D., & Ross, E. (1984). *Teaching reading in today's elementary schools* (3rd ed.). Boston, MA: Houghton Mifflin.

Byrd, I. (2011). *Differentiating within a gifted classroom.* Retrieved from http://www.byrdseed.com/differentiating-within-a-gifted-classroom

Catron, R. M., & Wingenbach, N. (1986). Developing the potential of the gifted reader. *Theory Into Practice, 25,* 134–140.

Clark, B. (1979). *Growing up gifted.* Columbus, OH: Charles E. Merrill.

Clark, B. (2002). *Growing up gifted: Developing the potential of children at home and at school* (6th ed.). Columbus, OH: Merrill Prentice Hall.

Cohen, C. (1997). *The effectiveness of peer coaching on classroom teachers' use of differentiation for gifted middle school students* (Unpublished doctoral dissertation). University of Connecticut, Storrs, CT.

Colangelo, N., Assouline, S. G., & Gross, M. U. M. (2004). *A nation deceived: How schools hold back America's brightest students* (Vol. 1). Iowa City: The University of Iowa, The Connie Belin & Jacqueline N. Blank International Center for Gifted Education and Talent Development.

Daneman, M. (1996). Individual differences in reading skills. In R. Barr, M. L. Kamil, P. B. Mosenthal, & P. D. Pearson (Eds.), *Handbook of reading research* (Vol. 2, pp. 512–538). Mahwah, NJ: Lawrence Erlbaum Associates.

Dole, J. A., & Adams, P. J. (1983). Reading curriculum for gifted readers: A survey. *Gifted Child Quarterly, 27,* 64–77.

Erickson, H. L. (2007). *Concept-based curriculum and instruction for the thinking classroom.* Thousand Oaks, CA: Corwin Press.

Fogarty, E. A. (2006). *Teachers' use of differentiated reading strategy instruction for talented, average, and struggling readers in regular and SEM-R classrooms* (Unpublished doctoral dissertation). University of Connecticut, Storrs, CT.

Fogarty, E. A. (2011). *Project rural: Differentiation.* Manuscript in preparation.

Gentry, M. L. (1999). *Promoting student achievement and exemplary classroom practices through cluster grouping: A research-based alterna-*

tive to heterogeneous grouping (RM 99138). Storrs: University of Connecticut, The National Research Center on the Gifted and Talented.

Greenlaw, M. J., & McIntosh, M. E. (1986). Literature for use with gifted children. *Childhood Education, 62,* 281–286.

Howell, H. (1985). *Literature, comprehension, and gifted readers.* Retrieved from http://eric.ed.gov

Jackson, N. E. (1992). Precocious reading of English: Sources, structure, and predictive significance. In P. Klein & A. J. Tannenbaum (Eds.), *To be young and gifted* (pp. 171–203). Norwood, NJ: Ablex.

Kaplan, S. (2001). An analysis of gifted education curriculum models. In F. A. Karnes & S. M. Bean (Eds.), *Methods and materials for teaching the gifted* (pp. 133–158). Waco, TX: Prufrock Press.

Kingore, B. (2004). *Differentiation: Simplified, realistic, and effective: How to challenge advanced potentials in mixed-ability classrooms.* Austin, TX: Professional Associates.

Kulik, J. A., & Kulik, C. L. (1991). Ability grouping and gifted students. In N. Colangelo & G. A. Davis (Eds.), *Handbook of gifted education* (pp. 178–206). Boston, MA: Allyn & Bacon.

Lee, H. (1960). *To kill a mockingbird.* New York, NY: J. B. Lippincott & Co.

Levande, D. (1999). Gifted readers and reading instruction. *CAG Communicator, 30,* 19–20, 41–42.

Marion, L. M. (1982, September). *A differentiated program in reading for gifted/talented.* Paper presented at the Annual Meeting of the Plains Regional Conference of the International Reading Association, Omaha, NE.

National Reading Panel. (2000). *Teaching children to read: An evidence-based assessment of the scientific research literature on reading and its implications for reading instruction.* Retrieved from http://www.nichd.nih.gov/publications/nrp/upload/smallbook_pdf.pdf

Parker, J. P. (1998). *Instructional strategies for teaching the gifted.* Boston, MA: Allyn & Bacon.

Reis, S. M. (2009). *The joyful reading resource kit: Teaching tools, hands-on activities, and enrichment resources*. San Francisco, CA: Jossey-Bass.

Reis, S. M., Burns, D., & Renzulli, J. S. (1992). *Curriculum compacting*. Mansfield Center, CT: Creative Learning Press.

Reis, S. M., Eckert, R. D., Schreiber, F., Jacobs, J., Briggs, C., Gubbins, E. J., . . . Muller, L. (2005). *The Schoolwide Enrichment Model reading study* (RM 05214). Storrs: University of Connecticut, The National Research Center on the Gifted and Talented.

Reis, S. M., Gubbins, E., J., Briggs, C., Schreiber, F. J., Richards, S., Jacobs, J., . . . Alexander, M. (2003). *Reading instruction for talented readers: Case studies documenting few opportunities for continuous progress* (RM 03184). Storrs: University of Connecticut, The National Research Center on the Gifted and Talented.

Reis, S. M., Gubbins, E. J., Briggs, C. J., Schreiber, F. J., Richards, S., Jacobs, J., . . . Renzulli, J. S. (2004). Reading instruction for talented readers: Case studies documenting few opportunities for continuous progress. *Gifted Child Quarterly, 48,* 315–338.

Reis, S. M., Little, C. A., Fogarty, E. A., Housand, A. M., Housand, B. C., Sweeny, S. M., . . . Muller, L. M. (2010). *Case studies of successful Schoolwide Enrichment Model–Reading (SEM-R) classroom implementations* (RM 10240). Storrs: University of Connecticut, The National Research Center on the Gifted and Talented.

Reis, S. M., Westberg, K. L., Kulikowich, J. K., Cáillard, F., Hébert, T. P., Plucker, J., . . . Smist, J. M. (1993). *Why not let high ability students start school in January? The curriculum compacting study* (RM 93106). Storrs: University of Connecticut, The National Research Center on the Gifted and Talented.

Reis, S. M., Westberg, K. L., Kulikowich, J. M., & Purcell, J. H. (1998). Curriculum compacting and achievement test scores: What does the research say? *Gifted Child Quarterly, 42,* 123–129.

Renzulli, J. S. (1977). *The Enrichment Triad Model: A guide for developing defensible programs for the gifted and talented.* Mansfield Center, CT: Creative Learning Press.

Renzulli, J. S. (1994). Teachers as talent scouts. *Educational Leadership, 52*(4), 75–81.

Renzulli, J. S., & Reis, S. M. (1985). *The Schoolwide Enrichment Model: A comprehensive plan for educational excellence.* Mansfield Center, CT: Creative Learning Press.

Renzulli, J. S., & Reis, S. M. (1997). *The Schoolwide Enrichment Model: A comprehensive plan for educational excellence* (2nd ed.). Mansfield Center, CT: Creative Learning Press.

Richards, S. (2003). *Current reading instructional practices for average and talented readers* (Unpublished doctoral dissertation). University of Connecticut, Storrs, CT.

Richards, S. (2008, July). *Supporting the high potential reader, writer, and thinker.* Paper presented at Confratute, Storrs, CT.

Rogers, K. B. (1991). Training teachers of the gifted: What do they need to know? *Roeper Review, 11,* 145–150.

Terman, L. M. (1925). *Mental and physical traits of a thousand gifted children: Genetic studies of genius* (Vol. 1). Stanford, CA: Stanford University Press.

Tomlinson, C. (1999). *The differentiated classroom: Responding to the needs of all learners.* Alexandria, VA: Association for Supervision and Curriculum Development.

VanTassel-Baska, J. (Ed.). (2008). *Alternative assessments with gifted and talented students.* Waco, TX: Prufrock Press.

VanTassel-Baska, J., & Brown, E. F. (2001). An analysis of gifted education curriculum models. In F. A. Karnes & S. M. Bean (Eds.), *Methods and materials for teaching the gifted* (pp. 93–132). Waco, TX: Prufrock Press.

Westberg, K. L., Archambault, F. X., Jr., Dobyns, S. M., & Salvin, T. J. (1993). *An observational study of instructional and curricular practices used with gifted and talented students in regular classrooms* (RM 93104). Storrs: University of Connecticut, The National Research Center on the Gifted and Talented.

Wingenbach, N. G. (1983). *A study of gifted readers: Metacognition and use of comprehension strategies* (Unpublished doctoral dissertation). Kent State University, Kent, OH.

Appendix A

The Gifted Reader's Bill of Rights

By Bertie Kingore

- The right to read at a pace and level appropriate to readiness without regard to grade placements.
- The right to discuss interpretations, issues, and insights with intellectual peers.
- The right to reread many books and not finish every book.
- The right to use reading to explore new and challenging information and grow intellectually.
- The right for time to pursue a self-selected topic in-depth through reading and writing.
- The right to encounter and apply increasingly advanced vocabulary, word study, and concepts.
- The right to guidance rather than dictation of what is good literature and how to find the best.
- The right to read several books at the same time.
- The right to discuss but not have to defend reading choice and taste.
- The right to be excused from material already learned.

From *Differentiation: Simplified, Realistic, and Effective: How to Challenge Advanced Potentials in Mixed-Ability Classrooms* (Appendix D), by B. Kingore, 2004, Austin, TX: Professional Associates.

Appendix B

Independent Work Contract

Student's Name: ______________________________

Guidelines for Independent Work

Student should:

- Have all materials ready
- Have his/her work schedule
- Be on task
- Avoid directing attention to himself/herself

Description of Replacement Activity(s):

____

____

____

____

____

____

____

____

Due Date: ______________________________

Teacher/Student Conference Dates:

____

Student's Signature: ______________________________

Teacher's Signature: ______________________________

Appendix C

Reading Interest-A-Lyzer

READING INTEREST-A-LYZER©

Based on the Interest-A-Lyzer by Joseph S. Renzulli

Name ______________________

Grade ______________ Age ________

1.) When I read for pleasure, I pick the following (Check all that applies):

- ☐ Novels/chapter books
- ☐ Sports books
- ☐ Poetry books
- ☐ History books
- ☐ Biographies
- ☐ Cartoons/comic books
- ☐ Newspapers
- ☐ Fantasy books
- ☐ Science books
- ☐ Other
- ☐ Humorous books
- ☐ Magazines
- ☐ Mystery books
- ☐ Scary books

2.) If I were in charge of my reading/language arts class, I would have any students do 10 of the following activities (Check 10):

- ☐ Write a story
- ☐ Write a book
- ☐ Write a poem
- ☐ Write a newspaper article
- ☐ Talk about a book with a friend
- ☐ Write a play
- ☐ Give a speech
- ☐ Read a favorite book again
- ☐ Read a challenging, new book
- ☐ Tell a story
- ☐ Make a cartoon or comic
- ☐ Learn a different language
- ☐ Listen to someone read aloud
- ☐ Learn sign language
- ☐ Create a game or puzzle
- ☐ Learn about an author or illustrator
- ☐ Read a poem
- ☐ Write the story of your life (autobiography)
- ☐ Draw/illustrate a story or poem
- ☐ Read a true story
- ☐ Read a biography or autobiography
- ☐ Read a crossword or other word puzzles
- ☐ Work on a crossword or other word puzzles
- ☐ Read a book aloud
- ☐ Watch a play/movie of a book that you have read (Spanish, French)
- ☐ Write a story about someone's life (biography)

3.) I am most likely to read a book for pleasure that:

- ☐ A teacher suggests
- ☐ A librarian suggest
- ☐ Is by an author whose books I have read
- ☐ My friend suggests
- ☐ Has won an award
- ☐ I just happened to see (hear about) in ____________________

4.) Three favorite books that I would take on a month-long trip are:

1. ____________________
2. ____________________
3. ____________________

5.) In the past week, I have read for at least half an hour (30 minutes):

☐ No days ☐ 1-2 days ☐ 3-4 days ☐ 6-7 days

6.) In the past month, I have read __________ book(s) for pleasure:

☐ No books ☐ 1-2 books ☐ 3-4 books ☐ 5-7 books ☐ 8 or more books

7.) My favorite time to read for pleasure is:

- ☐ Never
- ☐ During school
- ☐ Lunchtime
- ☐ In the evening
- ☐ Whenever I can
- ☐ In the morning before school
- ☐ During the midmorning
- ☐ After school
- ☐ Before falling sleep
- ☐ ____________________

8.) When I read I like to: ☐ read one book ☐ juggle more than one book at a time

9.) I like to receive books as presents. ☐ **YES** ☐ **NO**

10.) I view books a presents. ☐ **YES** ☐ **NO**

11.) I have a library card. ☐ **YES** ☐ **NO**

12.) If I read a book that I like, I am likely to read more books by the same author. ☐ **YES** ☐ **NO**

13.) If I read a book that I enjoy, I am likely to read more books about that topic. ☐ **YES** ☐ **NO**

14.) I borrow books from the library:

☐ Once a week ☐ Twice a week ☐ A couple of times a month
☐ Every few months ☐ A few times a year ☐ Hardly ever
☐ Never

15.) The number of books I have at home:

☐ None ☐ Less than 10 ☐ 11-20
☐ 21-30 ☐ 31-40 ☐ Too many to count

16.) If I could meet any literary character (for example, Laura from *Little House on the Prairie*, the Lion from *The Wizard of Oz*, Harry from *Harry Potter*, Curious George, Arthur, Babar) I want to meet:

- ____________________
- ____________________
- ____________________

17.) Where is your ideal reading spot?

☐ Bedroom ☐ Living room ☐ Family room
☐ Public library ☐ Kitchen ☐ Bookstore
☐ Car ☐ Home library ☐ Other ____________

18.) The last three books that I have read are:

1. ____________________
2. ____________________
3. ____________________

Note. From *The Joyful Reading Resource Kit* (pp. 131–133), by S. M. Reis, 2009, San Francisco, CA: Jossey-Bass. Copyright 2009 by John Wiley & Sons. Reprinted with permission of Sally Reis.

Appendix D

Booklists for Gifted Readers

Booklists on the Web

American Library Association
http://www.ala.org

Carol Hurst's Children's Literature Site
http://www.carolhurst.com

Notable Social Studies Trade Books for Young People
http://www.socialstudies.org/notable

Outstanding Books for the College Bound
http://www.ala.org/ala/yalsa/booklistsawards/outstandingbooks/outstandingbooks.htm

Outstanding Science Trade Books for Students K–12
http://www.nsta.org/publications/ostb

Planet Esmé
http://www.planetesme.com

Suggested Books for Gifted Readers Grades K–8

Table D1 contains a list of suggested books for gifted readers in grades K–8.

Table D1
Suggested Books for Gifted Readers in Grades K–8

Book Title and Description	Appropriate for Grades	Gifted Characters or People Are Present in the Book	Genre	Topics or Theme(s)
Among the Hidden (Margaret Peterson Haddix, 2000) This is the story of Luke, who was born during a time when having more than two children was illegal, forcing him to live a life in hiding. He must decide to what degree he will disobey in order to have freedom.	4–7		Science fiction	Justice, free will, totalitarianism
Anne Frank: The Diary of a Young Girl (Anne Frank, 1953) This is a must-read book for any adolescent wanting to understand the Holocaust from the perspective of the victims. Anne's story, however, will show readers that all humans experience love and fear.	5–8	•	Biography	Discrimination
Bad Beginning, The (Lemony Snicket, 1999–2006) This is the first book in a 13-book series that manages to entertain and teach advanced vocabulary in the context of three orphans' adventure to save their fortune and evade the evil Count Olaf.	2–5	•	Fiction	Vocabulary development, good versus evil, humor
Belle Prater's Boy (Ruth White, 1996) Cousins Gypsy and Woodrow experience the difficulties of small-town life in Virginia as a shroud of mystery envelopes their family after the disappearance of Woodrow's mother.	3–5	•	Fiction	Justice, morality
Best-Loved Doll, The (Rebecca Caudill, 1965) This sweet story of a girl's love for her doll is reminiscent of *The Velveteen Rabbit*. Both stories show readers the meaning of sacrifice in understandable terms.	K–3		Fiction	Love, sacrifice

Table D1, continued

Book Title and Description	Appropriate for Grades	Gifted Characters or People Are Present in the Book	Genre	Topics or Theme(s)
Bridge to Terabithia (Katherine Paterson, 1977) A boy and girl find friendship despite their differences. Through his friendship, Jess is encouraged to be himself and must also learn to cope with the loss of his friend. (Newbery Medal Winner, 1978)	3–6	•	Fiction	Friendship, individuality
Bud, Not Buddy (Christopher Paul Curtis, 1999) Bud is an orphan with the will and skills for survival, even when the odds are against him. Set in the Great Depression and the 1930s, the historical backdrop of this novel provides an education; the writing will evoke compassion. (Newbery Medal Winner, 2000)	3–5		Fiction	Prejudice, discrimination
Charlotte's Web (E. B. White, 1952) Pigs, spiders, and humans—we are all mortal. Some day we will all die. Therefore, we must spend our time on this Earth carefully and cherish friendships. Wilbur and Charlotte teach the reader this lesson in a book on friendship and the preciousness of life.	1–4	Gifted pig? Read to find out!	Fiction	Friendship, commitment, mortality
Chocolate War, The (Robert Cormier, 1974) Jerry Renault battles evil and struggles with his identity in a high school full of students of privilege.	6–8	•	Fiction	Justice, friendships, peer pressure, evil
Escape! The Story of the Great Houdini (Sid Fleischman, 2006) This book is the biography of Houdini, a man of magic. It is set at the turn of the century, and readers will see how the life of this famous man coincided with important historical events.	6–8	•	Biography	Magic, science investigation, history

Table D1, continued

Book Title and Description	Appropriate for Grades	Gifted Characters or People Are Present in the Book	Genre	Topics or Theme(s)
Flowers for Algernon (Daniel Keyes, 1959) A young boy with an IQ of 68 is given the gift of intelligence—a mixed blessing when he finds out that friends have been making fun of him. (Hugo Award for Science Fiction, 1959)	6–8		Science fiction	Mortality, limitations
From the Mixed-Up Files of Mrs. Basil E. Frankweiler (E. L. Konigsburg, 1967) Two children run away from home to live at The Metropolitan Art Museum in New York City and discover an artistic mystery. (Newbery Medal Winner, 1968)	3–5	•	Fiction	Independence
Giver, The (Lois Lowry, 1993) This book takes readers to a Utopian society where only the main character experiences emotion. (Newbery Medal Winner, 1994)	4–8	•	Science fiction	Memory, pleasure versus pain
Golden Compass, The (Philip Pullman, 1995) This myth-like book is one part of a trilogy featuring struggle for love and loyalty in a world that is both like and unlike our own. Although the main character grows up at Oxford, she does so with a daemon (animal that embodies the spirit), witches, and terrifying creatures.	5–7	•	Fiction	Loyalty, morality
Green Book, The (Jill Paton Walsh, 1982) This book is an environmental novel—it gives us a look at the direction in which our planet is headed and in the end it is the young people who save the society.	3–6		Fiction	Environmentalism

Table D1, continued

Book Title and Description	Appropriate for Grades	Gifted Characters or People Are Present in the Book	Genre	Topics or Theme(s)
Hobbit, The (J. R. R. Tolkien, 1937) Enter Tolkien's fantasy world and learn about good and evil from elves, hobbits, and dwarves.	3–8		Fiction	Fantasy, courage, good versus evil
House of the Scorpion, The (Nancy Farmer, 2002) In a society of "eejits," or people whose brains have been replaced by computer chips, Matt is special. He is pampered and taken care of. He soon learns that he is a slave of a different sort—he is a clone.	4–8	•	Science fiction	Courage, free will
House on Mango Street, The (Sandra Cisneros, 1991) Cisneros' lyrical and moving vignettes show the life of a Latina girl growing up in Chicago. At times the topics are mature (pregnancy, language) but these give a fuller picture to the life described within.	6–8	•	Fictional short stories	Family, culture
Hundred Dresses, The (Eleanor Estes, 1944) A class of girls learns compassion when they learn that their classmate did have 100 dresses in her closet—each of which was beautifully drawn.	1–3		Fiction	Kindness, compassion, poverty
I Am the Cheese (Robert Cormier, 1977) Adam Farmer's life is turned upside down when he finds out that his whole life is a lie. Lack of self-identity may be a theme that adolescents can identify with as they read about Adam's experiences.	6–8	•	Fiction	Loss, courage, self-identity

Table D1, continued

Book Title and Description	Appropriate for Grades	Gifted Characters or People Are Present in the Book	Genre	Topics or Theme(s)
Island of the Skog, The (Steven Kellogg, 1973) When mice friends leave the city, they have to deal with the only island inhabitant—the skog! The mice must pull together to solve their problem and stay safe. Critical and creative thinking are shown throughout this book.	K–2		Fiction	Cooperation, compromise
Joyful Noise: Poems for Two Voices (Paul Fleischman, 1988) This nature poetry was created for two readers. These poems are wonderful tools for introducing young students to the beauty of language and poetry. (Newbery Medal Winner, 1989)	1–3		Poetry	Nature
Little Women (Louisa May Alcott, 1868) This is the story of the triumphs and hardships of Josephine March and her family as she struggles to find her place in the world.	4–8	•	Historical fiction	Family, independence, Civil War, overcoming hardships
Long Way From Chicago, A (Richard Peck, 1997) Peck tells the stories of Grandma Dowdel through the eyes of her two grandchildren, Joey and Mary Alice. Set in the Depression, the reader will see the wit and humor of Peck in every Grandma Dowdel action, as well as the strength and character of the people of that time period.	3–6		Historical fiction	Family
Magic Tree House Series (Mary Pope Osborne, 1992–present) This series of books is good for the younger reader because although they are repetitive, they encourage hypothetical thinking, which is usually not yet strongly developed in children of this age.	K–3		Fiction	Adventure, cooperation

Table D1, continued

Book Title and Description	Appropriate for Grades	Gifted Characters or People Are Present in the Book	Genre	Topics or Theme(s)
Maniac Magee (Jerry Spinelli, 1990) A young boy unites a racially divided town after running away from home. (Newbery Medal Winner, 1991)	3–6		Fiction	Racism, poverty, friendship
Nothing But the Truth (Avi, 1991) A student perceives that his teacher is stifling his right to free speech and the two enter into a very public showdown. This book illustrates democratic principles and will have the reader empathizing with the teacher by the end.	4–7	•	Fiction	Justice, free speech
Number the Stars (Lois Lowry, 1989) This book shares a young girl's quest to save her best friend during the Holocaust. (Newbery Medal Winner, 1990)	4–7	•	Historical fiction	Holocaust, World War II, friendship, courage, tolerance
Outsiders, The (S. E. Hinton, 1967) In this coming-of-age novel, Hinton depicts the complicated coexistence of love, jealousy, and friendship in the teenage characters.	6–38	•	Fiction	Peer pressure
Phineas Gage: A Gruesome But True Story About Brain Science (John Fleischman, 2002) This book tells the story of Phineas Gage, who was either a very lucky or unlucky man when he didn't die when a railroad stake went through his skull. We continue to learn about the brain from Phineas even though he has been gone for many years.	5–8		Nonfiction	Human body, amazing events

Table D1, continued

Book Title and Description	Appropriate for Grades	Gifted Characters or People Are Present in the Book	Genre	Topics or Theme(s)
Roll of Thunder, Hear My Cry (Mildred D. Taylor, 1976) Set during the Great Depression, this book portrays the horror of slavery throughout history. (Newbery Medal Winner, 1977)	4–6		Historical fiction	Slavery, family, hope
Running Out of Time (Margaret Peterson Haddix, 1995) When a diphtheria epidemic breaks out, her mother is forced to tell Jessie that the family has been living in an 1840 preservation village unbeknownst to the children. Slipping out of the settlement and into modern times, Jessie learns of a devastating plot to kill the members of the village. This is an excellent book for talented readers due to the historical references and need for hypothetical thinking while reading.	3–6		Fiction	Justice, equality
Secret Garden, The (Frances Hodgson Burnett, 1911) Sullen children Mary and Colin find a secret garden and their dispositions change as they begin to care for the garden. They begin to live more fully as they learn that life is full of ups and downs, but the one constant is love.	2–5		Fiction	Love
Surviving the Applewhites (Stephanie S. Tolan, 2002) When Jake is kicked out of his last school, he comes to live with a family of artists and E.D., the only member of the family who is not artistic. Together, the two struggle to adapt to the family and each other.	3–6	•	Fiction	Adapting, misfits

Table D1, continued

Book Title and Description	Appropriate for Grades	Gifted Characters or People Are Present in the Book	Genre	Topics or Theme(s)
Voice That Challenged a Nation: Marian Anderson and the Struggle for Equal Rights, The (Russell Freedman, 2004) Freedman chronicles the life of singer Marian Anderson who became a crusader for civil rights the day she sang at an outdoor concert from which she had been banned.	4–6	•	Biography	Courage, civil rights
Way Things Work, The and *New Way Things Work, The* (David Macaulay, 1988, 1998) These books are for the curious. The author explains the workings of gadgets and technology complete with rich descriptions, interesting comparisons, and clear illustrations.	2–6		Nonfiction	Engineering
When Zachary Beaver Came to Town (Kimberly Willis Holt, 1999) Toby befriends Zachary whose mother earns money by charging people admission to their trailer to see the overweight boy. Toby's experiences with Zachary allow him to put his own life into perspective and realize that things aren't so bad.	4–6		Fiction	Empathy, obesity, social justice, morality
Wrinkle in Time, A (Madeline L'Engle, 1962) Meg, her brother, and her best friend go on an adventure full of wonder when they meet an extraordinary creature during their search for her father. (Newbery Medal Winner, 1963)	3–6	•	Science fiction	Mythology, courage, honor, fantasy
Year Down Yonder, A (Richard Peck, 2000) This book continues the story of Joey, Mary Alice, and Grandma Dowdel from *A Long Way From Chicago*. Peck manages to expand Grandma's character so that she is more crazy than ever—hysterically funny! (Newbery Medal Winner, 2001)	3–6		Historical fiction	Family

About the Author

Elizabeth A. Fogarty, Ph.D., is assistant professor of elementary education at East Carolina University in Greenville, NC, where she teaches both elementary education and gifted education classes. She obtained a master's degree in talent development and gifted education from Minnesota State, Mankato and a Ph.D. in educational psychology from The University of Connecticut focusing on gifted education. Her research interests include talented readers, differentiation, and teacher effectiveness. Dr. Fogarty is on the board of directors of the North Carolina Association for the Gifted and Talented and serves as the Professional Development Network Chair of the National Association for Gifted Children. She was named the 2010 Early Leader of the same organization.

Printed in the United States
by Baker & Taylor Publisher Services